Also by Ron Domen

Poetry

The Owl in the Woodwork (Finishing Line Press, 2017)

PLAINTIVE MUSIC

poems by

Ron Domen

DOS MADRES

2017

DOS MADRES PRESS INC.
P.O.Box 294, Loveland, Ohio 45140
www.dosmadres.com   editor@dosmadres.com

Dos Madres is dedicated to the belief that the small press is essential to the vitality of contemporary literature as a carrier of the new voice, as well as the older, sometimes forgotten voices of the past. And in an ever more virtual world, to the creation of fine books pleasing to the eye and hand.

Dos Madres is named in honor of Vera Murphy and Libbie Hughes, the "Dos Madres" whose contributions have made this press possible.

Dos Madres Press, Inc. is an Ohio Not For Profit Corporation and a 501 (c) (3) qualified public charity. Contributions are tax deductible.

Executive Editor: Robert J. Murphy

Illustration & Book Design: Elizabeth H. Murphy
www.illusionstudios.net

Typset in Adobe Garamond Pro & Dali
ISBN 978-1-939929-90-7
Library of Congress Control Number: 2017952228

Cover: Charles E. Burchfield (1893-1967), "Wind-blown Asters", 1951, watercolor on paper, 30"x40", collection of the Burchfield Penney Art Center, gift of Dr. Edna M. Linderman, 1968. Reprduced with permission of the Charles E. Burchfield Foundation.

First Edition

ACKNOWLEDGEMENTS

Grateful acknowledgement is made to the editors of the following publications in which some of these poems (some in slightly different form) first appeared:

Anemone: Wooden Ties; Studying Medicine in Guadalajara, Mexico: 1971-1975 (section number 7 as, Mexican Housecall)
Black Bear Review: Asphalt Man
Earth First!: Caterpillars
The Endless Mountains Review: A Winter's Day
Grasslands Review: Natural History
Green Fuse Poetry: Frogs
Mediphors: Studying Medicine in Guadalajara, Mexico: 1971-1975 (section number 5 as, The Mexican Village)
Mulberry Journal: Cannon's Bar
Pacific Coast Journal: Cutting Wood with my Son
Potato Eyes: Turning Wood
Riverwind: The Owl in the Woodwork
Slant: Sightseeing
Slipstream: The Steel Pail
Tributaries: Woodturner; Rockweed
Whiskey Island Magazine: Odyssey
Wildflower: Research (as, Painful Presence); Willie B.
Wild Onions: Snowbound; Snow; Conception; Steel Mill; Bottomland; First Rain; Armadillo; Studying Medicine in Guadalajara, Mexico (sections 1-4, 6, and 8); Tinnitus; Plaintive Music; Airport Fantasy; On Buying Our Gravesites; Highway Blues; Stone Steps
Yarrow: Pawnee Earth Lodge

"Herbal Tea" appeared in *The Flutes of Power* edited by Walt Franklin, Great Elm Press, Rexville, New York, 1995.

"Cannon's Bar" and "Research" (as, "Painful Presence") also appeared in *Pudding Magazine #23*, Pudding House Publications, Johnston, Ohio, 1994.

"Frogs" also appeared in *Cattle Bones & Coke Machines: An Anthology of Poems Examining the Impact of Humanity on the Earth's Energy Systems,* Smiling Dog Press, Maple City, Michigan, 1995.

"Beaver Creek" appeared in *Voices of Cleveland: A Bicentennial Anthology of Poems by Contemporary Cleveland Poets*, Cleveland State University Poetry Center, Cleveland, Ohio, 1996; and in, *I Have My Own Song For It: Modern Poems of Ohio,* edited by Elton Glaser and William Greenway, The University of Akron Press, Akron Series in Poetry, Akron, Ohio, 2002.

"Odyssey" also appeared in *Cityscape*, edited by Bonnie Jacobson and Leonard Trawick; a publication in the "Poetry: Mirror of the Arts Series," sponsored by the Poets' League of Greater Cleveland, Cleveland, Ohio, 1996; and, was staged and performed by actors at the Cleveland Museum of Art, Cleveland, Ohio, on June 5, 1996, as part of the Cleveland Museum of Art's special exhibition *Transformations in Cleveland Art, 1796-1946.*

"Words" appeared on the website: http://www.poetsagainstthewar.org

"Conception" also appeared in *Hektoen International: A Journal of Medical Humanities,* Volume 2, Issue 3; Fall 2010 (Published by the Hektoen Institute of Medicine, Chicago, Illinois).

"Plaintive Music" also appeared in *Hektoen International: A Journal of Medical Humanities*, Volume 4, Issue 3; Fall 2012 (Published by the Hektoen Institute of Medicine, Chicago, Illinois).

The Found Poems are from; *Charles Burchfield's Journals: The Poetry of Place.* Edited by, J. Benjamin Townsend. Albany: State University of New York Press, 1993.

Several of these poems appeared in the chapbook, *The Owl in the Woodwork* (Finishing Line Press, Georgetown, KY; February 2017; ISBN: 978-1-63534-140-9)

My thanks to the poets Christopher Bursk, Patricia Goodrich, and Cortney Davis, and the late Len Roberts, for help and encouragement along the way, and to the *Virginia Center for the Creative Arts* for a fellowship that provided me space and solitude in which some of these poems were written or conceived. Special thanks to my wife, Kate, for her critical reading of my work, and her never-ending support and encouragement.

for Kate

TABLE OF CONTENTS

In geological terms
we all have the same measure of immortality…
The days are stacked against what we think we are.

-        Jim Harrison

All my life I have yearned for some strange land
of poetry and imagination…
If you would be a poet, express the poetry of nature…
Most people see nature
only through the eye of a great poet or artist.

-        Charles Burchfield

Beaver Creek

—for Charles Burchfield (1893-1967)

"...the voice of the turtle
is heard in our land..."
-- Song of Solomon 2:12 (KJV)

There was a time when flowers
had thoughts and the hills heard
turtles speak of the brilliant colors
of things growing and butterfly
festivals and cricket fantasies
of red hepaticas and windblown
asters on sultry summer afternoons.
When fog lingered in late morning
light instead of escaping to Post's
Woods or Trotter's Swamp along
Little Beaver Creek you stopped
by the empty barn and sheds
at the end of an alley forsaken
and mournful as the coal mines
and coke ovens that surrounded
your small Ohio town.
You painted the hard buildings
and splendid trees with heavy
strokes of raw sienna and ocher
yellow and black never failing
to show the *strange white light*
that hovered around the edges.

1

Odyssey

—for Charles Burchfield (1893-1967)

The hot wind blew
and grasshoppers
bounded in waves
across dry fields.
Inside your studio
light fluttered
around the edges
of your canvas
and the stuffed
crows scowled
from their perches.
A mysterious gloom
settled on everything.
You hungered
for perpetual
summer days wandering
Ohio woodlands
and ravines
discovering clumps
of hepaticas or flocks
of blackbirds flitting
across meadows.
Outside your window
brilliant sunlight struck
with a thundering howl
and splashed over
the red barn
and white birches.

The Owl in the Woodwork

—for Charles Burchfield (1893-1967)

I soared over darkened
fields and feasted
on mice.
As the sun rose
over the hill
I plunged
into the dusky woods
to avoid the blinding
light and became lodged
between two young
white pines.
We grew together
and my eyes turned
to knots
my blood to sap
my body to wood.
Then a thunderous
splintering and buzzing
as a jagged disk
cut through me.
I hate this light.

Found Poem: Cicada Woods

—for Charles Burchfield (1893-1967)

The hot white drought wind
comes out of the brassy south-
west sky scorching the earth
with its breath like a blast
of air from a coke oven small
saplings shrivel and stand gaunt
with curled dry white leaves
grass is brittle and dry hundreds
of grasshoppers and locusts zig-zag
through the maze of stems white
glaring sunlight dances in waves
the air full of the continuous tick-tick-tick
and zee-zee sounds of countless insects
shattered at times by penetrating
metallic songs of cicadas.

Found Poem: A Rainy Day

—for Charles Burchfield (1893-1967)

The moist air holds the smoke
prisoner and the breeze carries
it idly about mingling it
with its own steamy breath
until we cannot tell which is which;
thoughts and movements are softened
an absence of sunlight
bird and insect songs
all things swell –
the earth, plants, wood
and even iron –
we must expand like the leaves.

Found Poem: The Far North

—for Charles Burchfield (1893-1967)

Out of the north from lowering
skies fall whirling flakes
of snow falling among the dry leaves

where are hepaticas snowdrops and crocuses.
They come from the far north
Where there are deep ravines

with dark pine recesses and caves
under overhanging slaty ledges
where lurk masses of greenish

ice seemingly centuries old
from them a cool breath proceeds
into the cavernous hollows

between the steep banks a passing
wind sweeps dry leaves
from the top banks in a dizzy

whirl swaying the branches
of pines these catch a stray glint
from the pale March sun

the black shadows of prehistoric
fear lurk under ledges under
pines in the caves under logs

from the remote sunlight world
outside comes a mysterious call
of a distant bluebird.

The Steel Pail

—for my father

The cherry wood burns
to a pile of gray-white
ashes but not before
it fills the room
with the sweet smell
of itself and releases
to the fire blues
oranges and reds locked
somewhere inside.
As a boy you climbed
the cherry tree
now neatly stacked
in the woodpile
and collected the tart
dark red fruit
in a gray steel pail.
But no matter
what you gathered
the path always led back
to that three-roomed
miner's shack with bitter
and pungent smells
of kerosene lamps
and woodsmoke
to a mother who would
not talk and a father
who left bloody coal-flecked
phlegm in a coffee can
next to the potbelly stove.

Turning Wood

—for my father

I watch him bent
over his wood lathe
with heavy coat on
and hood drawn tight
around his face.
In the garage woodshop
a kerosene heater
blows hot air
to remove winter's chill.
No gloves on his hands
so the fingers can feel
when the wood has been
shaped and smoothed
as only he knows.
The wood block
spins a blur
shavings fly up from
the tool in his hands
and cling to eyebrows
lenses of glasses
and to the hair on
the back of his hands.
Hands that for forty
years cut and spliced
electrical wire in order
to pay the way.

Wooden Ties

For twenty years I listened to the lull
of freight trains lumber through
my Ohio neighborhood.
Ponderous bulks twisted past
farms and small towns
as the commerce of the country
pressed its weight on steel rails
sprung from mills in Pittsburgh,
Youngstown, and Cleveland.
Steel mills that ground dirt
into my father's skin until
pumice soap and a brush
barely sufficed.

Intermingled with new Fords from Detroit
and hundred-year old western timber
were open cars filled with coal carried
from Appalachian mines on the backs
of men who sat next to potbelly stoves
on straight-backed chairs
and coughed up coal dust.

The railroad ripped up the tracks
and his steelworker's pension was lost
but today I helped my father place
five wooden railroad ties to mark
the boundaries of his new garden.

Bottomland

On the path to the creek
where the widow tends
her garden a copperhead
sliced with a hoe shrivels
in the morning heat
as cicadas drone from oaks
and maples around the three
roomed miner's shack.
Piles of gray slate on
surrounding hillsides mark
abandoned coal mines worked
to exhaustion or sealed shut
as tombs against underground
fires and the men trapped inside.
While the outhouse slowly
slips into the ravine
kerosene lamps fill rooms
with flickering shadows
and across the hollow comes
the whippoorwill's dusky call.

Woodturner

This birch log on the lathe I saved
from a campfire in the north woods
as we drank neat Scotch whiskey
from blue enameled cups
while coyotes yipped
in the surrounding blackness.
A loon swam ahead of our canoe
and an eagle squawked from atop
a white pine before it swooped
low over the lake.

Now I gouge and scrape
at the accumulated years of growth
layered around the bowl hidden
inside this spinning birch log
as bits and pieces fly from the tool
in my hands and cling tenaciously
to skin and hair until the white
grain streaked blue and brown
with minerals nursed from the earth
glows like the veined translucent
skin of a newborn child.

First Rain

No rain for months
but on an April
afternoon we watch
from the doorway
as heavy drops
from fast moving gray-
black clouds beat
back the yellow dust
thickening on everything
like a callus.
You hug my neck
tight and lean into
the rain as far
as you dare your
free hand trying
to catch and hold
the rain before it
falls to the ground
our smiling faces wet
from the warm mist-
laden wind.

Cutting Wood with my Son

The gun-barrel blue sky
gave way to an orange sun
as the white puffs
of our breath floated
up and trailed behind.
I carried the chainsaw
and gasoline and you
the oil can with both hands.

I cut dead trees while you
sat on a log with knees
pulled up under your chin
and chattered from your perch
like some blue-coated
red curly-haired bird.

Loading logs into the pickup
truck you wanted to wear
my gloves but they kept
falling off so you braved
the cold air and rough
and splintered wood
with bare hands.

Woodsmoke

A cold November rain studded
with flurries strips the final
skin of leaves and lays bare
the bones of trees to bring it all
back to stark simplicity once
again like this oak library
table where I write that was carried
by the B&O from Pittsburgh
to my great grandmother's Ohio
parlor almost a hundred years
ago this winter when my father
and I strip off the dark aged
varnish and sand smooth
the deep grained honey-colored
wood until the accumulated
crust of a century gathers
around our feet and the wood
dust covers our clothes and sticks
tenaciously to our hair.
Not until my father lays down
a new skin of varnish caressing
the oil deep into the raw oak
with his bare bony hands
does it finally come back
to its pure and marvelous
and ordinary self like the clean
smell of woodsmoke that comes
out of nowhere from an unknown

hearth on a winter day
when I breathe deep drafts of it
into my lungs until it becomes
part of my own steamy breath
visible in the frost-laden air.

Studying Medicine in Guadalajara, Mexico: 1971-1975

It is estimated that there are presently 3,715 American-born students who are forced to study medicine in a foreign country, in a foreign tongue.

-Donald D. Goldberg, MD;
Journal of the American Medical Association,
May 12, 1975

1

Crossed the Rio Grande River
at Laredo, Texas turned south
on Mexico highway 85
and made for Sabinas Hidalgo
a crossroads with a Pemex
gas station and restaurant
and luckily a first rate auto mechanic
who stayed late for the single
malt scotch whiskey intended
for the journey's end but more
than half gone by the time
I returned with the needed parts
from a junk car dealer in Laredo
riding the bus into the late evening
with workman just back from the fields
and factories the sweat and dirt staining
their shirts and the caged chickens
cocking their heads and clucking.
The commingling smells
of animal, hard toil, and sweet
desert sage are no stranger

than this white kid from Ohio
standing in the bus with a tangled
mass of metal drum and spindle
and bearing and brake parts
that faith tells me will replace
the Buick's worn out left front
wheel assembly while from the back
of the bus a goat bleats.

2

Monterrey and then past the abandoned
boxcars outside of Saltillo turned into houses
without windows and last gas
at Concepción del Oro
before crossing two hundred miles
of desert and climbing into the mountains
to Zacatecas and another two hundred
miles of mountain road to Guadalajara
"the Queen City" five thousand feet high
in the Valley of Altemajac south
of the Tropic of Cancer along the old volcanoes
of the Sierra Madre Occidental.
Spent Saturday night in the Holiday Inn.
Register for classes on Monday.

3

A late night walk in the deserted
streets when the rattletrap '57 Chevy ambulance
came down Avenida Mariano Otero
popping and backfiring past that venerable

priest's statue and sputtered to a complete
stop with its American tourist heart
attack in the back along with the wife
and her brother.
No oxygen or drugs or IV's
and no machines to shock the heart
back to life only bare hands
pushed on his chest to start
it beating once again.
Each successful resuscitation soon
followed by failure until nothing
worked and another ambulance
finally came to make the trip
to the funeral home.

4

Operated on stray dogs
to learn how to cut and sew.
Went down to the kennels
each week for a semester to pick one
and carry it to the operating room.
The dogs stink and piss
all over us and shake
like they know that
they will be sacrificed in the end.
We were required to wear all white.

5

The canvas cots in the sacristy
of the Catholic church
with the broken windows
in Ocotlán was home for two weeks.
Some of us went door-to-door
to find the sick and some
waited behind small wooden
tables in open courtyards.
I saw a young woman
who wanted pills because
twenty-two pregnancies
was surely enough –
even for the Pope.
But please doctor don't
tell my husband.
I saw an old man who lay
pale and weak in a room
where the windows had
no glass and the floor
was hard red-brown dirt.
How did he bear
the mosquitoes at night?
Chickens scratched in
the dirt at the bedside
and cocked their heads
at patient and doctor
as if they understood.

6

Driving back to Guadalajara
after a summer break in the States
the car's water pump blew
outside of the town of Jerez
and was replaced by another first
rate auto mechanic.
Courtyards hid behind brick
walls capped with broken
glass and the men back
from pushing plows in the fields
stand at the bar and suck on limes
and rock salt drinking beer and shots
of tequila with the urinal trough
at their feet and the whole time
their straw hats still on
as if the oppressive sun
of four hundred years
could find them in that place.
Past wet laundry strung
across the hallway the night
spent in a cot-sized bed.

7

I walked past the turkeys
pecking around the yard
and the goat tied at the door.
A crucifix hung on
the adobe wall above
a small wooden table

where a single candle burned.
A chicken scratched the dirt
floor around a bed in
the corner where a girl
coughed bloody bits
of her lungs
into a tin can.

8

Bodies floated in a tank of formaldehyde
and when one was needed an assistant
snagged it with a long hooked pole
and pulled it out dripping to a marble table.
They waited for us in rows and most
were headless because a professor wanted
to know more about the brain and dissected
the heads for himself.
We picked away at muscles
learned points of origin and insertion
followed the course of nerves
and arteries located the heart behind
the bony breastplate and each day scraped
and peeled away more flesh until nothing
was left to dissect and only
the bones remained.

Belated Letter to a Mother

I remember that night over thirty years ago as if it was yesterday. I was the internal medicine resident on-call and fresh out of my internship and responsible for evaluating all potential admissions to the medicine service. Although your son was four years old I was asked to assist in his care because the pediatric resident was not comfortable taking care of your son's critical injuries. The pediatric resident certainly blind-sided me that night but that was the reality back then in our inner city hospital that did not have a pediatric intensive care unit and where staffing and finances were often stretched. I am not making excuses but simply stating the facts. The ambulance that came to your house should have taken your son to University Hospitals even though it would have meant a longer ride but there is little value in rehashing every decision that was made that night – although, I admit that I have done so many times. When I arrived in the emergency room your son was already in critical condition. A breathing tube had just been inserted and he was connected to a respirator. The concern was that his heart might stop at any moment and after I examined your son I agreed that he was too critically ill to be transported to another hospital. We would simply have to do the best we could under the circumstances. I don't know what transpired between you and your boyfriend that day, but I do know that your son somehow got caught in the middle, and only you knew where the bright line of truth was and how he came to suffer such bruises to his head and small body. I knew that it was no simple fall down the stairs and I noted my suspicions in his medical chart. I was too busy caring for your son to personally talk to

23

you for any length of time, and in those days physicians felt that domestic violence was more a matter for social workers and the police. I guess that I assumed that the medical record would make its way to the proper people, who would make the appropriate assumptions and follow ups, and that connecting the dots was out of my hands. Of course, that sort of protective thinking has gone by the wayside and we would like to think that we are more enlightened about such things today. Your son was placed in the adult intensive care unit, and I have to admit, it was a little odd having him there because his small body looked out of place among patients who had mostly lived long and full lives and who were in the ICU for the usual adult things like strokes, heart attacks, or bad lung disease from years of working in the coal mines or from smoking too many cigarettes. Your son's injuries turned out to be far worse than I first suspected and all of our limited tests back then showed that his brain was well along the road to permanently shutting down to the outside world. When I threaded a needle between his backbones and examined the spinal fluid that bathed his brain it was full of blood and the pressure was sky high. By the time the neurosurgeon got there the balance had tipped for the worst and surgery was not an option. I gave him steroids in a weak attempt to decrease the brain swelling in the hope that some visible life might come back into those beautiful, dark brown eyes. It wasn't long until his heart became more and more erratic and his blood pressure more difficult to control. Throughout the night I gave him drugs to correct one or the other but it wasn't long before his kidneys also started to fail and I knew that, pending a miracle, it would only be a matter of hours before his young body gave out. As the night wore on my bedside vigil became one of simply being there – bearing witness and providing comfort – rather than one of medical necessity. I continued to make feeble attempts to alter the course his brain and body had irrevocably taken – at least my machinations made me feel as if I was doing something to help – but by dawn his heart had given up for good and I turned off the machines. Please believe me when I tell you that I gave your son the best that I had in me, and I hope that you can take some comfort in that; but, I admit, it has been only scant comfort for me. I don't recall thinking much about the fact that you were notably absent, and given the circumstances, perhaps I thought you were with the police. I didn't want to face the possibility that you were not there because you simply did not care whether your son lived or died. I am writing this belated letter in the hope that you did care, that it could have been otherwise, and for the realization that most of my career had to pass before I was able to commit these words to paper. You failed your son and I fear that we – the whole wobbly system – failed both of you. It is easy, in hindsight, to make excuses but we also had to learn, and we are still working at it. Are you still working at it? What have you learned? I have learned over these thirty-plus years that there still are no simple answers or solutions for many of the medical and social ills we practitioners of the healing art continue to face. That sometimes all we can do is what the poet does – "to see, to hear, to feel" – and more times than not, it is enough. I only hope and pray that you have come to appreciate that no one deserves to suffer at the hands of another and that there are alternatives and safe places to go to and that there are trustworthy people out there who truly care and who want to help. I made a private vow that I would not let my own discomforts and fears get in the way of overcoming such barriers. Your son was one of the first to teach me that hard-earned lesson. I hope he has taught you as well.

Research

I first noticed it as a boy
when I killed the hummingbird -
I didn't stop to admire the way
it hovered at the flower's mouth.

I operated on stray dogs
to learn surgery.
I practiced cutting down
through skin, muscle and
the almost transparent membrane
covering coils of intestines.
Little knots of thread carefully
tied to stop the bleeding.
Usually the dogs were not
allowed to wake up.

In the next lab cats were
strapped to wood planks.
Backs were cut open to expose
fragile spinal cords so that
calculated weights and forces
could be delivered.

For my research I needed
bone marrow cells.
I would stick a large needle
into the dog's hip bone
and suck out bits of marrow.
After awhile it shook
and cowered when
I came near.

Leukemia

—for Kyle (April 8, 1982 to April 9, 1990)

At first I didn't know what it meant
to have bad blood cells and that
I would have to go to the hospital.
Last year another boy in my school
had leukemia and he got real sick.
No one saw him for a long time
then someone said he had died
and we never saw him again.

I've known about death, really.
I had plants that turned brown
and died and once I had goldfish
and one-by-one my mom helped me bury them.
Every year there were men in
the neighborhood who went into the woods
and came back with dead deer tied
to their cars their eyes stuck open
like big glass marbles.

At first I felt ok but the pills
made me sick and I lost my hair.
I threw up a lot and sometimes
there was blood and my face got puffy
and funny looking and sometimes
my bones and tummy hurt.
Once I caught mommy and her
friend holding each other and crying
and then trying not to when I came around.

When I first went to the hospital the nurses
all came around and we laughed
and I got lots of neat cards and letters.
Each time I went back fewer friends
came to see me and no one sent cards
or toys and it got harder to laugh.

I thought about death
but I had trouble talking about it.
I got so weak and just laid around
and the pains got worse
and the fevers make me shake.
Then I shook because I was afraid.
I didn't know what was happening
and no one would talk to me
even though I wanted to know more.
I liked the touches and having my back
rubbed and my head stroked
but my hair kept falling out.

So this is what it is to die?
I hate you all and I hate
what I look like.
I hate this needle in my arm
that you keep pushing drugs
into but the morphine helps
the pain.
No, I don't really hate you.

I love you and I'm sorry
that I got sick and made you sad.

I tried to get better and waited
for my birthday.
It was a great party.
I wish that I could hug and kiss
you but I am so very weak
and all I want to do is close
my eyes and never be sick again.
But my eyes are open and I can't see.

Tinnitus

*The ringing in your ears
is the cricket in the stars.*

—Gary Snyder

A chronic ringing sound in the ears
when there is really no sound to be heard.
It's all in your head, a constant pathological
reminder of too many rock concerts
or perhaps one more vestige from those
jackhammer steel mill days. It often means
impending deafness like my father suffers,
or worse, the cry of a brain tumor making
itself known. The inability to recall memories
is a side effect. This may explain why I can't
remember the names of long ago lovers.
Does it matter that I have forgotten names,
dates, and circumstances; or that it might
have been otherwise, but probably not?
And if by some miracle the ringing should
stop will a cloud of lost memories break
through like the sun slowly burning off
a foggy morning, or will they come
suddenly like an unexpected phone
call from an old friend?

Steel Mill

Greek and Slovak immigrants with grime
from greasy sludge pits imbedded deep
under fingernails and in hard calluses
went through the barred gate year
after year with my father and walked
phlegm spotted passageways and learned
to name things in a new language
while turning pig iron into steel.
Horns blared from blast furnaces
great doors lifted and hot malleable
masses of steel bounced down narrow
gauge tracks to the rolling mill spewing
white-yellow sparks that in seconds could burn
deep into unprotected skin or eye.
In the hospital a deaf steelworker
who lost both legs when steel fell
from an overhead crane and broke
his back taught us to speak
with our hands.

Armadillo

I

I remember the armadillo
that rooted in my Florida yard
poking its pointed snout
under layers of grass and dirt
in its hunt for ants or scorpions
while in our search for common
ground we scratched and scraped
at shells as bony and rigid
as the armadillo's knowing
that the naked underside is soft
and escape the only defense.

II

In Cannon's Bar in Allentown
a stuffed armadillo is propped
against an old copy of *Gray's
Human Anatomy* the book
I studied in medical school to learn
what actually lies under thick
layers of skin and how the heart
hides behind the breastplate.

Natural History
—for M.B.

We walked through the Pharaoh's tomb
brought to Chicago three thousand
years after masons cut the massive
stone blocks out of the earth.
Next to his two mummified children
we talked of the burden of being
part-time fathers and felt the weight
of disagreeable compromises.
In the Hall of Mammals we sat
on a wooden bench and spoke
about your upcoming surgery
and the relief it might bring while
the two man-eating lions of Tsavo
stuffed and posed glared
from glass enclosed natural splendor.

Stone Steps
—for Sue C.

Hidden among the frosted brown
grass and brambles along
this familiar back road
only these abandoned stone
steps mark the absent house
like a headstone where
in the dark corners and closets
of your buried childhood you
would be awakened in the night
by the rough and callused hands
that pinned you tight like a butterfly
in a glass case until he had his way.
But on this gray spring morning
voices sing the familiar hymns
in the white clapboard church
next to the cemetery where names
have weathered off the stones
and are forever lost to their children's
children and over the empty field
a murder of crows swoops close
and the hardwoods creak
in a cool breeze laden with the crisp
smell of mock orange.

Plaintive Music

On that day in waning winter
as the sunrise spread red-orange
and purple like a bruise only

the brightest star Sirius could still
be seen pulsating like the dot
of heart on the sonogram

of our unborn child wrapped
in ariled darkness before it too
disappeared in the morning light.

Now in the last days of summer
newly hatched cicadas brown-red
as blood clots rise from grounded

dormancy on journeys marked
by liturgical drones until their bronzed
chitinous skin becomes too tight

to hold such plaintive music
and splits to leave behind empty
hard-shelled wombs.

Conception

It is important to know the stories
that surround our conception.
But leave out the part about the hormone
surge that expands the cumulus cells
surrounding the zona pellucida
and prepares the egg for fertilization.
I would rather know if there was passionate
love-making in the back seat of a Ford
at a drive-in movie the rolled up windows
made opaque from your steamy breaths.

And don't go into detail how sperm
must fight their way through fibrous
macromolecules in cervical mucus
to get to fallopian tube fimbria
where the egg awaits fertilization.
Tell me about the gibbous moon
that rose above the swell of waves
on your honeymoon beach
and like sea turtles hatching
out of the sand and making their way
back to salt water I too
started my journey there on the sand.

And don't use medical terms like capacitation
or hyperactivation to describe how sperm
must penetrate the zona pellucida
in order to fertilize the egg.
I want to know the details of how
the fog-laden air hung lanuginous

and misty in the park's twilight
and dew on the grass mixed
with the lustrous sweat on your bodies.

And if you start to tell me about
sperm crossing the egg's equatorial
segment and membrane fusion followed
by cleavage and embryo implantation
I will wonder about the outside drone
of traffic mingling with the radio's music
in your bedroom as shadows from streetlights
streaked across the bed and the sound of me
came like the rustle of clothes dropped
to the floor around your feet.

Pawnee Earth Lodge

*"And the noise of the geese
remembers the promise."*
—Pawnee Legend

In a Chicago museum I enter
a replica of a lodge and feel
the calm of hewn timber
clods of dirt and grass
the smoothness of lost
corners and sharp angles.
A firepit lies below a hole
in the domed roof and in
the west under the hanging
sacred bundle which contains
things of the earth a buffalo
skull sits upon an altar.
This house is not more than
a bubble on the surface of nature.
Where does one start
and the other end?
The door always faces east
to catch the rising sun
and the fire is in the center.

Asphalt Man

—for Loren Eiseley (1907-1977)

The dead yield their secrets
through layers of dirt
and flesh turned to ash
and white bony skulls
with empty sockets
that no longer see.
The bones warn us that
only confusion lies
in mass-produced daydreams
that truth is not reached
by sleek and fast highways
where asphalt man blindly
walks the road laid
down by the dead.
But the dead tell us
to look to the past
to see inside ourselves
for the future.

Cannon's Bar

Let's walk to the corner tavern
where we will eat boiled
corned beef and cabbage
and drink a beer beneath
the stuffed armadillo and The Indian
caught alive in a photograph
of the long wooden bar.
We will hold hands and tap
our feet on the plank floor
to the Irish tunes of ancestors
never forgotten in that long
journey from Dublin to Allentown.
Later I will take you and you
will take me and together
we will resurrect the dead.

Herbal Tea

A Ruby-throated
hummingbird hovers
over a scarlet
pompon of Bee-balm
sucking nectar
the minty leaves
used long ago
by Oswego Indians
to make tea.

Willie B.

Captured from lowland
forest under African skies
where you played free
and learned things gorilla
to a small cement room
in the Atlanta Zoo.
Twenty-seven years
not allowed sunshine
shade of tree
squish of earth
between toes.
Your world a carousel
of faces.

A new exhibit
with grass and sky
remote and hostile
to your hesitant steps.

Caterpillars

The fog finally lugs
itself from the meadow
leaving behind Red-winged
blackbirds to ramble
through grasses
and hardwood saplings
heads bobbing
as they peck for bugs
in brown dirt.
Clusters of white
flowered Yarrow
fill gaps between
the road and useless
fence the rotting
posts returning
to soil like the old
man who farmed
this land.
Down the road
yellow Caterpillars
belch and snort
from their smoky
engines as they claim
and reshape these fields.

Frogs

Radioactive leopard
frogs born from toxic
uterine mud behind
Oak Ridge National
Laboratory leap
like lambent fugitives
down highway sixty-two
to become radiant
amphibian clots
plastered on tires
of cars and trucks
dashing through the night.

Rockweed

In thick fog harbor
seals and cormorants sit
on white-stained rocks
of Egg Rock Island
where the unmanned
lighthouse flashes
every thirteen seconds
while floating green-brown
rockweed mats together
in mile-long tendrils
that scavenge the sea's
surface for plastic bottles
styrofoam cups and rubber
ducks lost from passing ships
or dropped by walkers
along the shore path
while from the sunny summit
of Cadillac Mountain it is possible
to see how perfectly fog fills
the hollow of Frenchman's Bay.

Sightseeing

We rode motorcycles
through Appalachian coal
towns coursing veinlike
along hilly back roads.
We slept by a haystack
pistol in your hand
in case of intruders.

At a gas station
an old lady
spoke of the peace sign
on my helmet
as a broken cross
a sign of the devil
while gunshots echoed
in the valley
as a boy pretended
a glass bottle
was the enemy.

In a small Virginia town
we stopped at a gunshop
to sell the .45-caliber
semi-automatic Argentinean pistol.
We needed cash more
than a false sense of security.
The shop was long and narrow
built in the last century
the outside of wood
grain heavy and deep
from decades of weather.

The wood floor
was worn smooth
by generations
of fathers and sons.
A KKK poster
on the wall.
The owner stroked
and rolled the gun
felt its weight
sighted down its length
pulled the trigger.
I'll give you fifty dollars.

Words

They sharpen their tongues like swords
and aim their words like deadly arrows.
　　　　　—Psalm 64:3 (NIV)

Smooth tongued recruiters hone
their words like a sword
and parade through our schools

in slick military uniforms
and talk of honor duty patriotism
and festive occasions to welcome

home (living) heroes.
No speeches recount pains
in phantom limbs or wheelchairs

driven with a joystick
in the mouth or the realization
that God does not choose sides.

There are no anthems for those
who refuse the call to arms
who listen instead to the inner

hum of the blood that courses
through the veins of all men.
Blessed are the peacemakers

who search for new words
to speak a new language
and a taste of peace.

Snow

on this first morning
of the year and eleven inches
already cover the ground.
Only a few weeks ago the wild
geese ran in waves across
the field in front
of the children who thought
they could herd them into flight.
But the geese stayed until
the lake began to freeze
then like a frustrated spouse
lifted off south in a burst
of flapping wings
and clamorous honks.

A Winter's Day

At my feet lay
dead brown leaves
partially covered by
patches of melting snow.
Overhead
two trees grow
so close together
that the wind plays
the creaking music
of tree rubbing against tree.

Snowbound

On this barely above zero
snow crunch under boot
January morning sparrows
scrunch beneath the under-
brush into ruffled feathery
balls and huddle like home-
less men on subway grates
and nothing moves in icy
hush except hardwoods
that creak in scant wind.

Northern Wisconsin

The creek flows from the lake
and meanders through peat

bog and scrub pine past ghosts
of great and venerable trees.

A loon plies the glassy water
and the sun dips behind

quaking aspens with leaves
tinged orange and yellow

that shimmer in the placid dusk
while in the east a gibbous moon

rises over the ridge and coyotes
yip in the growing dark.

At the Beach

The humid heat holds me
like a beetle on a pin
as the sun bears down
with the force of an exploding
nova until it feels as if flames
will spring spontaneously
from the white-hot sand
as my greased flesh sizzles
and turns red like a Maine
lobster in a pot of boiling water
the fight for life lost.

Seagull Dance

Over the bay
a long line
of seagulls ride
a vortex of air
in great expanding
circles that spiral
to an imaginary
pinnacle until
disillusioned
by what is not
there each dancer
breaks free
to glide alone
back to earth.

Lake Ada

—for Mike and Barb

We could ride this canoe all night
across the lake's mirrored face
and play tag with the moon's
reflection.

Remember when we stood tall
and expectant next to the pines
in the morning mist and made our vow?
We are as free as this floating island
and as hopeful as that fish jumping up
through the darkness trying
to catch the moon.

Airport Fantasy

In a few hours I could be
at a fresh point of departure –
Seattle, Houston or Miami
beckon as quiet ports
as I walk down the concourse.
Flight 53 to Charleston
is now boarding through gate 12.
It would be so easy.
Memphis, Billings or maybe
Los Angeles – now there's
a black hole city one can drop
into and never stop falling.
To board a different flight
and watch the sun set
behind a new horizon
learn the names of new streets
grow a beard and make new
friends and better choices.
But who can truly run away?
I arrive at my designated gate
and take my assigned seat –
my seatbelt fastened tight
in case of turbulence.

Highway Blues

As the car courses
through an early
autumn afternoon
the palpable silence
between us becomes
an unwanted passenger
as unspoken words
try to come together
to explain the hurt
and anger.
Through the window
a lone tree with golden
leaves shines bright.

Ars Poetica

The process of tearing down
and putting back together
that requires a willing

and sacrificial prostration
before the gods who watch
over the holy and evil parts

with vision to see
the whole of its parts
with the inner eye's pupil

constricting and dilating along
infinite angles balancing
on the focal point and sighting

back along fuzzy edges
with the focus of religious
imagination and inspiration

only to walk in murky molecular
darkness and suffer beyond
what seems real until you feel
the fire at its center.

Fog

Our lives
are like the fog
that comes
in the night
only to vanish
with the sunrise.

On Buying Our Gravesites

The living know that they will die,
but the dead know nothing…
—Ecclesiastes 9:5 (NRSV)

Snow begins to fall once again
on this windswept knoll along
the Lehigh River where the black

bony trees and dark gravestones
dot the slope of Nisky Hill
and the crisscross tracks

of small animals about their early
morning business are visible
in the whiteness.

We stand on the eastern portion
of the northern one-half of lot
two in section G and survey

the nearby family names etched
in granite where our corporeal selves
will huddle among oaks and sycamores

in shared hallowed dirt
the affairs of earth like Cezanne's
black clock with no hands.

ABOUT THE AUTHOR

RON DOMEN is a physician in south central Pennsylvania where he is a Professor of Pathology, Medicine, and Humanities, and a former Associate Dean, at the Penn State Hershey Medical Center and College of Medicine. He was born in rural Ohio and grew up in the industrial northeastern part of Ohio. He obtained his undergraduate degree from the Youngstown State University and his MD degree from the Universidad Autonoma de Guadalajara (Mexico).

Author Photo by Kate Domen

For the full Dos Madres Press catalog:
www.dosmadres.com